From 9-5 to Thriving Entrepreneur

The Mission Mindset - Shaping Your Destiny as an Entrepreneur

Side Hustle Series

Book 2

R. Fredimann

Author: R. Fredimann

Editor: Blissfulplan Publishing Ltd.

Title: From 9-5 to Thriving Entrepreneur: The Mission Mindset - Shaping Your Destiny as an Entrepreneur

Series: Side Hustle

Volume 2

To you who struggle to find enough motivation to escape the rat race!

"Build your own dreams, or someone else will hire you to build theirs."

— Farrah Gray

Contents

Introduction

Welcome to "The Mission Mindset: Shaping Your Destiny as an Entrepreneur," a comprehensive guide designed to equip you with the knowledge, strategies, and insights necessary to thrive in the entrepreneurial world. This volume is a journey through the core aspects of entrepreneurship, meticulously structured to build your understanding from the ground up and transform your vision into tangible success. From cultivating the right mindset to navigating the intricacies of market dynamics, branding, and value proposition, each chapter is a stepping stone towards realizing your entrepreneurial aspirations.

In Chapter 1, we explore the foundational entrepreneurial mindset, essential for anyone embarking on this journey. Understanding your 'Why', as discussed in Chapter 2, sets the stage for purpose-driven entrepreneurship. Setting ambitious goals the SMART way in Chapter 3, coupled with developing resilience and grit in Chapter 4, prepares you to face the challenges ahead with courage and determination. Mastering time management, as outlined in Chapter 5, ensures that you make the most of your most precious resource. Navigating risk and uncertainty in Chapter 6 teaches the art of strategic decision-making, while Chapter 7 emphasizes the power of building a solid network for support and growth. Defining your target market in Chapter 8 and creating a compelling brand in Chapter 9 are crucial steps for aligning your offerings with your audience's needs. Finally, Chapter 10 delves into crafting an irresistible value proposition, the cornerstone of your entrepreneurial venture's success.

Chapter 1

Understanding the Entrepreneurial Mindset

The journey of an entrepreneur is often filled with both excitement and uncertainty. It requires a unique set of characteristics and a mindset that can shape one's destiny. In this chapter, we will explore these essential qualities and delve into the mindset necessary for success as an entrepreneur. Whether you are a student, marketer, aspiring entrepreneur, early-stage entrepreneur, side hustler, career changer, personal development enthusiast, or a social and environmental change maker, understanding the entrepreneurial mindset will serve as a guiding light on your path to success.

Passion and Purpose:

At the core of the entrepreneurial mindset lies an unwavering passion and purpose. Successful entrepreneurs are driven by a deep-rooted desire to make a difference and create a positive impact in the world. They are fueled by a passionate belief in their ideas and are willing to go above and beyond to bring their vision to life.

This passion helps entrepreneurs overcome obstacles, withstand setbacks, and persevere through the inevitable challenges that come their way. It fuels their motivation and enables them to inspire others to join their mission. Without passion and purpose, the entrepreneurial journey becomes a mere transactional pursuit of profits, devoid of meaning.

Embracing Risk:

Entrepreneurs are risk-takers. They understand that building something new and innovative involves stepping out of their comfort zones and taking calculated risks. They are willing to take a leap of faith and explore uncharted territories, even when failure seems imminent.

Risk, for an entrepreneur, is not a deterrent but an opportunity for growth. They see it as an essential part of the journey towards success, as each setback and failure serves as a valuable lesson to pivot, adapt, and move forward. It is this willingness to embrace risk that sets entrepreneurs apart from the crowd, allowing them to create groundbreaking ideas and transformative solutions.

Adaptability and Resilience:

In the ever-evolving landscape of entrepreneurship, adaptability and resilience become indispensable traits. Entrepreneurs must be able to navigate through uncertainty, adapt to changing circumstances, and make swift decisions when faced with unforeseen challenges.

The ability to pivot and embrace change is what propels entrepreneurs forward. They understand that flexibility and adaptability are necessary not only for survival but also for growth. Resilience serves as their armor, allowing them to bounce back from setbacks and keep moving ahead, undeterred by obstacles.

A Growth Mindset:

Entrepreneurs possess a growth mindset, which is rooted in the belief that their abilities can be developed through dedication and hard work. They view failures and mistakes as valuable opportunities for learning and improvement. Instead of being discouraged by setbacks, entrepreneurs see them as stepping stones towards greatness.

A growth mindset also enables entrepreneurs to continually seek knowledge, develop new skills, and evolve as individuals. They understand the importance of ongoing personal and professional growth and are committed to acquiring the necessary expertise to navigate the ever-changing entrepreneurial landscape.

Vision and Creativity:

Entrepreneurs are visionaries. They possess an innate ability to see opportunities where others see challenges. They have the capacity to envision a better future, identify problems that need solving, and create innovative solutions.

This visionary mindset also demands a certain degree of creativity. Entrepreneurs approach problems from unconventional angles and think outside the box to find unique solutions. They are not bound by conventional wisdom or limitations, and their imagination knows no bounds. Creativity is their superpower, allowing them to disrupt industries, challenge norms, and bring groundbreaking ideas to life.

In Conclusion:

The entrepreneurial mindset is a powerful force that sets entrepreneurs apart and propels them towards success. It is a combination of passion, risk-taking, adaptability, resilience, growth mindset, vision, and creativity. As we delve deeper into this chapter, we will explore each characteristic in detail, uncovering the secrets of the entrepreneurial mindset and how it can shape your destiny as an entrepreneur. So stay tuned and get ready to embark on an empowering journey of self-discovery and transformation.In the previous section, we explored the essential qualities and characteristics that form the foundation of the entrepreneurial mindset. We discussed passion and purpose, embracing risk, adaptability and resilience, a growth mindset, and the power of vision and creativity. Now, let us delve deeper into the intricacies of these traits and their significance in shaping your destiny as an entrepreneur.

Passion and purpose are at the heart of every successful entrepreneur's journey. Passion ignites the fire within, fueling the drive to overcome obstacles and the determination to bring ideas to life. It is the force that keeps entrepreneurs going during the most challenging times, pushing them forward when doubt starts to creep in. When you are deeply passionate about your vision and purpose, your commitment transcends mere financial gain or personal success – it becomes a genuine desire to make a positive impact on the world around you.

However, passion alone is not enough. The entrepreneurial journey is fraught with risks, uncertainties, and setbacks. This is where the willingness to embrace risk becomes crucial. Entrepreneurs understand that every risk taken is an opportunity for growth, innovation, and progress. They are not deterred by the fear of failure but rather see it as a stepping stone towards success.

By pushing past their comfort zones, entrepreneurs discover their true potential and unlock doors to new possibilities.

To navigate the ever-changing landscape of entrepreneurship, adaptability and resilience are indispensable qualities. The ability to adapt to changing circumstances, pivot when necessary, and make swift decisions in the face of uncertainty can determine the fate of a venture. It is through adaptability that entrepreneurs remain agile and stay one step ahead of the competition. Alongside adaptability, resilience serves as a sturdy armor that shields entrepreneurs from the inevitable setbacks and challenges. Being able to bounce back, learn from failures, and persevere is essential on the path to success.

A growth mindset is another vital characteristic that sets entrepreneurs apart. Entrepreneurs firmly believe that they can develop their skills and abilities through dedication and hard work. They view failures and mistakes not as roadblocks but as opportunities for learning and improvement. By approaching challenges with a growth mindset, entrepreneurs remain open-minded and continuously seek knowledge, honing their skills and expanding their expertise.

Vision, coupled with creativity, is a potent combination that propels entrepreneurs forward. Visionaries have the ability to see opportunities where others see challenges. They possess a unique perspective that enables them to identify problems, visualize a better future, and create innovative solutions. By thinking outside of conventional boundaries, entrepreneurs disrupt industries, challenge the status quo, and pave the way for groundbreaking ideas to flourish.

As we conclude this chapter, we have explored the essential characteristics and mindset necessary for success as an entrepreneur. Passion, risk-taking, adaptability, resilience, a growth mindset, vision, and creativity form the bedrock of the entrepreneurial journey. By cultivating these traits within ourselves, we can shape our destinies as entrepreneurs and create meaningful impact in the world.

Now, armed with a deeper understanding of the entrepreneurial mindset, it is time to reflect on your own aspirations and goals. Take a moment to assess your passions, interests, and the impact you want to make in the world. Consider the risks you are willing to take and the resilience you can cultivate. Embrace the power of a growth mindset to continually learn and evolve. Cultivate your vision and nurture your creativity.

Remember, the entrepreneurial journey is not a solitary one. Surround yourself with like-minded individuals who can support and inspire you along the way. Seek out mentors, connect with fellow entrepreneurs, and engage in communities that share your values and aspirations.

In the next chapters, we will dive deeper into the practical aspects of entrepreneurship, exploring strategies, tools, and frameworks that will further equip you on your path to success. But for now, take a moment to internalize the foundations we have discussed thus far. You possess the innate qualities and mindset essential to embark on this empowering journey of self-discovery and transformation.

Are you ready to shape your destiny as an entrepreneur? The journey awaits, and the possibilities are endless.

Chapter 2

Discovering Your Why

As an entrepreneur, understanding your true purpose and passions is crucial in shaping your destiny. It is the driving force that fuels your motivation, guides your decisions, and ultimately sets you apart on your entrepreneurial journey. In this chapter, we will delve into the process of identifying your personal mission and uncovering the why behind your entrepreneurial aspirations.

Before we embark on this discovery, it is important to recognize that finding your purpose is not an overnight revelation. It requires self-reflection, introspection, and a willingness to explore the depths of your being. It is a journey that may take time, but the rewards are undeniable.

The first step in this process is to explore your interests, hobbies, and talents. What activities make you lose track of time? What subjects or industries captivate your attention? Take a moment to jot these down and consider how you can align these interests with your entrepreneurial endeavors. Remember, finding your purpose is about incorporating your passions into your path as an entrepreneur.

Next, it is essential to examine your core values. What principles do you hold dear? What do you stand for? Consider the impact you want to make on the world and how your entrepreneurial pursuits can align with these values. By identifying your core values, you lay the foundation for a mission-driven mindset as an entrepreneur.

Furthermore, self-awareness is key in uncovering your purpose. Take time to reflect on your strengths, weaknesses, and personal experiences. Reflecting on your successes and failures can provide valuable insights into what drives you and what you are truly passionate about. Embrace moments of introspection and explore how these experiences have shaped your journey thus far.

In addition to self-reflection, seeking inspiration in the stories of others can be enlightening. Read books, listen to podcasts, and engage with mentors who have embarked on similar entrepreneurial paths. Learn from their experiences, challenges, and successes. By immersing yourself in these narratives, you expand your understanding of the possibilities and ignite a fire within you.

It is important to note that your purpose may evolve over time. As you gain experience and grow as an entrepreneur, your mission may shift or become more refined. Embrace this process of self-discovery and allow yourself the freedom to adapt and realign your path accordingly.

Beyond personal exploration, understanding the needs of your target audience is vital in discovering your purpose as an entrepreneur. Seek to identify the pain points and challenges faced by your potential customers. By addressing these needs, you can align your mission with the goals of your audience, ultimately creating a meaningful and impactful venture.

As you continue the journey of discovering your why, remember that it is not solely about financial gain or personal success. True purpose extends beyond oneself. It encompasses making a positive difference, leaving a lasting impact, and contributing to the greater good. By aligning your entrepreneurial endeavors with a greater mission, you not only find fulfillment but also attract like-minded individuals who share your vision and values.

In the second half of this chapter, we will delve deeper into how to translate your purpose into actionable steps and how to embody your mission mindset on your entrepreneurial path. But for now, pause, reflect, and let the insights from this first half guide you as you continue to uncover your true purpose as an entrepreneur.

Stay tuned for the next part of this chapter, where we explore the practical strategies and mindset shifts necessary to fully embrace your mission as an entrepreneur. Until then, let the journey toward discovering your why continue to unfold, igniting your passion and propelling you toward a purpose-driven entrepreneurial future.In the second half of this chapter, we will delve deeper into how to translate your purpose into actionable steps and how to embody your mission mindset on your entrepreneurial path. With a clear understanding of your why, it's time to take the necessary steps to bring your purpose to life and make a lasting impact.

One of the key aspects of embodying your mission is aligning your daily actions and decisions with your purpose. This requires intentionality and a commitment to staying true to your values. As an entrepreneur, it's easy to get caught up in the hustle and bustle of running a business, but it's important to regularly reassess if your actions are in line with your mission. Take the time to evaluate whether your choices are helping you fulfill your purpose and make the impact you desire.

A powerful tool in embodying your mission is creating a mission statement. This concise statement articulates your purpose, the values you uphold, and your goals as an entrepreneur. It serves as a guiding light, providing clarity and focus amidst the challenges and uncertainties of entrepreneurship. Take the time to craft a mission statement that resonates with you and reflects the impact you want to make. Keep it in a visible place and refer to it often as a reminder of your why.

As you progress on your entrepreneurial journey, it's crucial to surround yourself with a supportive network of like-minded individuals who share your vision and values. Seek out mentors, join communities, and attend networking events where you can connect with others who are passionate about making a difference. These connections can offer guidance, support, and inspiration, helping you stay motivated and accountable to your mission.

To fully embrace your mission mindset, it's important to redefine success on your own terms. As an entrepreneur, it's easy to fall into the trap of measuring success solely by financial gains or external achievements. However, true success lies in the fulfillment and impact you create. Take the time to define what success means to you personally and align it with your purpose. Celebrate not only the milestones and accomplishments but also the positive difference you're making in people's lives.

Adopting a growth mindset is another crucial aspect of embodying your mission. Embrace challenges as opportunities for growth and learn from both your successes and failures. Remember that setbacks and obstacles are part of the journey, but with a mission-driven mindset, you have the resilience and determination to overcome them. Continuously seek opportunities to learn, improve, and expand your knowledge and skills. Invest in your personal and professional development, as it will enhance your ability to make a meaningful impact on the world.

As you progress on your mission-driven entrepreneurial path, don't forget the importance of self-care. Nurturing your physical, mental, and emotional well-being is essential for maintaining balance and sustaining your passion. Prioritize self-care practices that fuel your energy and help you stay connected to your purpose. Whether it's exercise, meditation, spending time in nature, or engaging in creative activities, make time for activities that rejuvenate and inspire you.

In conclusion, discovering your why is just the first step in shaping your destiny as an entrepreneur. Embodying your mission requires intentional action, alignment with your values, and a commitment to continuous growth. It's about making choices and taking steps that are in line with your purpose, redefining success based on your impact, surrounding yourself with a supportive network, and practicing self-care. Embrace the journey of uncovering your true purpose and allow it to guide you toward a purpose-driven entrepreneurial future.

As we conclude this chapter, remember that your mission is unique to you. Stay true to your values, embrace your passions, and let your purpose be the driving force behind your entrepreneurial endeavors. The power to shape your destiny lies within you, fueled by a mission mindset that aligns your actions with your purpose. As you continue your journey, may you find fulfillment, make a positive impact, and forge a path that leaves a lasting legacy.

Chapter 3

Setting Ambitious Goals the SMART Way

Have you ever wondered how successful entrepreneurs seem to effortlessly achieve their goals? It almost seems like they have a secret formula or hidden skill that sets them apart from the rest. The truth is, they do have a mindset that drives them towards success, and it starts with setting ambitious goals.

Goal setting is a fundamental aspect of any entrepreneurial journey. It provides a clear direction, keeps you focused, and propels you towards your desired destination. However, not all goals are created equal. To ensure your goals are not merely dreams but actionable targets, you need to adopt the SMART framework.

SMART, an acronym for Specific, Measurable, Achievable, Relevant, and Time-bound, presents a systematic approach to goal setting. By incorporating these five essential elements, you can set yourself up for success and increase the likelihood of achieving your entrepreneurial aspirations.

The first element of SMART goal setting is specificity. And

no, we're not talking about vague and generalized goals like "make lots of money" or "be successful." Specificity is about clearly defining what you want to achieve. It involves answering the five Ws: who, what, when, where, and why. For example, instead of aiming to "start a business," a specific goal would be to "launch an e-commerce platform selling handmade jewelry by December 2024." By being specific, you can create a roadmap to guide your actions.

Once you have a specific goal in mind, it's time to make it measurable. Measuring progress not only allows you to track your success but also provides a sense of accomplishment along the way. To make your goal measurable, break it down into smaller, manageable tasks and set milestones. For our e-commerce example, you could set milestones such as creating a branding strategy, sourcing suppliers, and setting up an online payment system. By measuring your progress, you can stay motivated and adjust your approach if necessary.

While being ambitious is crucial for entrepreneurial success, setting goals that are too far-fetched can be demotivating and unattainable. That's where the third element of SMART goal setting comes in – achievability. Your goal should stretch your capabilities and push you out of your comfort zone, but it should still be within the realm of possibility. Assess your available resources, skills, and time to determine whether your goal is achievable. If it seems too overwhelming, consider breaking it down into smaller, more manageable steps.

Relevance is the fourth element of setting SMART goals. It's important to align your goals with your overall entrepreneurial journey and aspirations. Ask yourself how your goal contributes to your long-term vision. Does it bring you closer to your ultimate mission? If the answer is yes, then your goal is relevant. By ensuring relevance, you can maintain focus and avoid getting sidetracked by opportunities or distractions that deviate from your path.

Finally, time-bound goals create a sense of urgency and provide a clear deadline for achievement. Without a timeframe, goals tend to linger and lose momentum. Establishing a deadline holds you accountable, drives you to take action, and prevents procrastination. Going back to our e-commerce example, setting a specific launch date of December 2024 creates a sense of urgency and prompts you to work diligently towards that goal.

By following the SMART framework, you can set ambitious and achievable goals that propel your entrepreneurial journey forward. Specificity ensures clarity and direction, while measurability allows you to track progress and stay motivated. Achievability keeps your goals within reach, relevance ensures alignment with your overall vision, and time-bound goals create urgency and focus.

Now that you understand the importance of SMART goal setting, it's time to put this knowledge into practice. In the second half of this chapter, we will delve deeper into effective strategies and techniques to implement the SMART framework successfully. Stay tuned for valuable insights and practical tips that will revolutionize your goal-setting approach and help you shape your destiny as an entrepreneur. But for now, let's pause and leave you with this powerful framework to ponder upon. Remember, setting goals is not just about dreaming; it's about taking action and making your entrepreneurial aspirations a reality.In the second half of this chapter, we will delve deeper into effective strategies and techniques to implement the SMART framework successfully. By understanding and applying these techniques, you will be able to set ambitious and achievable goals that propel your entrepreneurial journey forward.

One effective strategy to implement the SMART framework is

to break down your goals into smaller, actionable steps. This allows you to create a clear roadmap and makes your goals less overwhelming. By breaking them down, you can focus on one step at a time, which not only increases your chances of success but also keeps you motivated along the way.

To break down your goals effectively, start by identifying the major milestones or key tasks that need to be accomplished. These milestones should be specific and measurable, aligning with the first two elements of the SMART framework. For example, if your goal is to launch an e-commerce platform selling handmade jewelry, your milestones could include creating a branding strategy, sourcing suppliers, and setting up an online payment system.

Once you have identified your milestones, you can further break them down into smaller, manageable tasks. These tasks should be actionable and time-bound, aligning with the last two elements of the SMART framework. For instance, under the milestone of creating a branding strategy, tasks could include designing a logo, defining your target audience, and developing a brand messaging guide. Setting deadlines for these tasks ensures that you stay on track and maintain a sense of urgency.

Another strategy to implement the SMART framework effectively is to regularly monitor and evaluate your progress. This allows you to make any necessary adjustments and keep yourself motivated. Consider keeping a journal or using a digital tracking tool to record your progress. Celebrate your achievements along the way, no matter how small they may seem. By acknowledging your progress, you will stay motivated and committed to achieving your goals.

Furthermore, it is important to remain flexible and adaptable as you work towards your goals. The entrepreneurial journey is filled with unexpected twists and turns, and your goals may need to be adjusted accordingly. Be open to reassessing your goals and modifying your action plan if necessary. Being flexible does not mean giving up or compromising on your ambitions; it means being willing to explore new opportunities and adjust your approach to ensure success.

Additionally, surrounding yourself with a support network can greatly enhance your chances of success. Seek out like-minded individuals, mentors, or accountability partners who share your entrepreneurial aspirations and can provide guidance and motivation. Collaborating with others who are on a similar journey allows you to learn from their experiences, gain valuable insights, and stay focused on your goals.

Finally, practicing self-reflection and staying aligned with your purpose is vital for achieving long-term success as an entrepreneur. Regularly assess whether your goals are still relevant to your overall vision and mission. As you grow and evolve, your goals may need to be adjusted to accommodate these changes. Take the time to reflect on your progress, reassess your goals, and ensure that they are aligned with who you are and what you truly want to achieve.

In conclusion, setting ambitious goals the SMART way is key to shaping your destiny as an entrepreneur. By incorporating the five elements of the SMART framework – specificity, measurability, achievability, relevance, and time-bound – you can set yourself up for success. Break down your goals into smaller, actionable steps, monitor your progress, remain flexible, seek support, and stay aligned with your purpose. Remember, goal setting is not just about dreaming, but also about taking action and making your entrepreneurial aspirations a reality. Let the SMART framework be your guide as you navigate the exciting and challenging path of entrepreneurship.

. . .

Now armed with valuable insights and practical tips, you are ready to implement the SMART framework and set ambitious goals that will propel your entrepreneurial journey forward. Whether you are a student, marketer, aspiring entrepreneur, early-stage entrepreneur, side hustler, career changer, personal develop-ment enthusiast, or social and environmental change maker, the SMART framework is a powerful tool that can revolutionize your goal-setting approach. So go forth, embrace the mission mindset, and shape your destiny as an entrepreneur.

Chapter 4

Developing Resilience and Grit

A s an entrepreneur, one of the most important qualities you can develop is resilience. The road to success is never smooth, and obstacles and failures are bound to occur. It is how you navigate through these challenges and bounce back that will ultimately shape your destiny. In this chapter, we will explore strategies to overcome obstacles, bounce back from failures, and cultivate resilience as an entrepreneur.

Resilience can be defined as the ability to adapt, recover, and grow stronger in the face of adversity. It requires mental toughness, perseverance, and a growth mindset. But how can you cultivate resilience in your own entrepreneurial journey? Let's explore some effective strategies.

1. Embrace a Positive Mindset:

Maintaining a positive mindset is crucial when faced with obstacles or setbacks. Instead of dwelling on failures, view them as opportunities for growth and learning. Reframe challenges as valuable experiences that can provide valuable lessons. By adopting a positive outlook, you can shift your focus towards finding solutions and moving forward.

2. Practice Self-Reflection:

Take the time to reflect on your past experiences and analyze them objectively. Identify the lessons you have learned, the mistakes you have made, and the strengths you have gained. Self-reflection allows you to develop a deeper understanding of yourself as an entrepreneur and helps you build resilience by recognizing your own capacity for growth and improvement.

3. Seek Support and Build a Network:

No successful entrepreneur achieves their goals alone. Surround yourself with a network of like-minded individuals who can offer support, advice, and encouragement. Connect with mentors, fellow entrepreneurs, and industry experts who can provide guidance and share their own experiences. Building a strong support system will not only help you during challenging times but also provide a sense of camaraderie and inspiration.

4. Develop Problem-Solving Skills:

Resilient entrepreneurs are skilled problem-solvers. They approach challenges with a solution-oriented mindset, searching for creative and innovative ways to overcome obstacles. Cultivate problem-solving skills by seeking out new perspectives, brainstorming ideas, and honing your critical thinking abilities. The more adept you become at finding solutions, the more resilient you will be when faced with adversities.

5. Embrace Failure as a Stepping Stone:

Failure is an inevitable part of entrepreneurship, but it is also a crucial stepping stone to success. Rather than viewing failure as a setback, view it as an opportunity to learn, grow, and improve. Embrace a growth mindset that sees failures as valuable feedback and stepping stones towards achieving your goals. The ability to bounce back from failures with renewed determination is a hallmark of resilience.

6. Cultivate Emotional Intelligence:

Emotional intelligence plays a vital role in resilience. It is the ability to recognize, understand, and manage your own emotions, as well as effectively navigate interpersonal relationships. By developing emotional intelligence, you can better cope with stress, setbacks, and conflicts. It allows you to adapt, maintain focus, and communicate effectively, even in challenging situations.

7. Set Realistic Goals:

Setting realistic goals is crucial for maintaining resilience. While ambitious goals can be motivating, setting unrealistic expectations can lead to disappointment and decreased resilience. Break down your larger goals into smaller, achievable milestones, allowing you to celebrate victories and stay motivated. This approach will help you maintain a sense of progress and resilience as you work towards your ultimate vision.

Developing resilience and grit as an entrepreneur is not an overnight process. It requires continuous effort, self-reflection, and a commitment to personal growth. By embracing a positive mindset, seeking support, developing problem-solving skills, and learning from failures, you can cultivate resilience that will propel you towards success.

Remember, Rome wasn't built in a day, and neither will your entrepreneurial journey. With resilience, determination, and an unwavering mission mindset, you have the power to shape your destiny as a successful entrepreneur.

In the second half of this chapter, we will delve deeper into the strategies that can help you develop resilience and grit as an entrepreneur. These strategies will equip you with the tools to face adversity head-on and continue on your journey towards success.

8. Practice Self-Care:

Taking care of yourself physically, mentally, and emotionally is essential for maintaining resilience. As an entrepreneur, it's easy to get caught up in the demands of building a business and neglect your own well-being. However, by prioritizing self-care, you can recharge and build the mental and physical stamina necessary to navigate the challenges that come your way. Make time for activities that bring you joy and relaxation. Engage in regular exercise, get enough sleep, eat nutritious meals, and practice mindfulness or meditation. By nurturing yourself, you'll be better equipped to handle the ups and downs of entrepreneurship.

9. Foster a Growth Mindset:

Cultivating a growth mindset is crucial for building resilience. A growth mindset is the belief that your abilities and intelligence can be developed through dedication and hard work. Embrace challenges as opportunities for growth, and see setbacks as temporary hurdles that can be overcome. By reframing your mindset, you can transform obstacles into valuable learning experiences and continue to progress towards your goals. Remember, it's not about where you start, but about your willingness to learn, adapt, and improve along the way.

10. Practice Emotional Regulation:

Entrepreneurship can be an emotional roller coaster, and it's important to be able to manage your emotions effectively. Develop strategies to regulate your emotions during times of stress or frustration. This could include deep breathing exercises, journaling, or seeking support from a trusted friend or mentor. By acknowledging and addressing your emotions, you can prevent them from derailing your progress and maintain a steady focus on your mission.

11. Embrace Adaptability:

Resilient entrepreneurs embrace change and adapt to new situations. In today's fast-paced world, businesses need to be flexible and open to evolving circumstances. By being adaptable, you can navigate shifting market trends, embrace new technologies, and seize opportunities as they arise. Stay curious, keep learning, and be willing to adjust your strategies based on feedback and new information. The ability to adapt is a key factor in long-term success as an entrepreneur.

12. Celebrate Small Wins:

Resilience is not only about bouncing back from failures but also about acknowledging and celebrating your victories along the way. Break your larger goals into smaller milestones, and take time to celebrate each achievement. Recognizing and rewarding your progress can boost your motivation and build resilience. It also serves as a reminder of how far you've come and reinforces your determination to keep pushing forward.

13. Learn from Mentors and Role Models:

Seek out mentors and role models who have experienced similar entrepreneurial journeys. Learn from their successes and failures, and tap into their wisdom and guidance. Find opportunities to network with experienced entrepreneurs through industry events, conferences, or online communities. Engaging with those who have walked the path before you can provide valuable insights, inspiration, and support. Mentors can offer advice based on their firsthand experiences and provide a perspective that can help you navigate challenges with more clarity and confidence.

14. Develop a Long-Term Vision:

Building resilience involves having a clear vision of the future you want to create. A compelling long-term vision provides a sense of purpose and drives your actions even when faced with obstacles or setbacks. Take the time to define your mission and values, and develop a strategic plan to achieve your vision. Having a clear direction will help you stay focused and persistent, even in the face of adversity.

15. Practice Gratitude:

Gratitude is a powerful tool for resilience. Taking the time to appreciate the positive aspects of your entrepreneurial journey, no matter how small, can boost your resilience and overall well-being.

Cultivate a gratitude practice by regularly reflecting on what you're grateful for. This simple exercise can shift your mindset, foster positivity, and strengthen your ability to bounce back from challenges.

Remember, developing resilience and grit as an entrepreneur is an ongoing process. It requires continuous effort, self-reflection, and a commitment to personal growth. By embracing these strategies and cultivating resilience, you will be equipped to overcome obstacles, bounce back from failures, and shape your own destiny as a successful entrepreneur.

In conclusion, building resilience and grit as an entrepreneur is essential for navigating the challenges and uncertainties of the entrepreneurial journey. By embracing a positive mindset, seeking support, honing problem-solving skills, and learning from failures, you can cultivate the resilience necessary to overcome obstacles and shape your own destiny. With determination, perseverance, and an unwavering mission mindset, you have the power to create your own success story. Keep pushing forward and never underestimate your ability to transform challenges into opportunities for growth and achievement. The journey may be tough, but the rewards are immeasurable.

Chapter 5

Mastering Time Management

Time management is an essential skill for entrepreneurs looking to navigate the fast-paced world of business. As an entrepreneur, your time is your most valuable asset, and how you manage it can significantly impact your productivity and success. In this chapter, we will delve into practical techniques and tools that will help you effectively manage your time and optimize your productivity. Whether you are a student, marketer, aspiring entrepreneur, or career changer, the strategies discussed here will empower you to take control of your schedule and shape your destiny as an entrepreneur.

The Importance of Time Management

Time management is not just about being efficient or productive; it is about making intentional choices that align with your goals, priorities, and values. When you master time management, you can maximize your output while minimizing stress and overwhelm. As an entrepreneur, you have numerous responsibilities and tasks vying for your attention, making effective time management a critical skill to develop.

By managing your time effectively, you can:

1. Accomplish More:

When you prioritize tasks and create an organized schedule, you can accomplish more in less time. By focusing on high-value activities, you can make significant progress towards your goals and grow your business.

2. Reduce Stress:

Having a clear plan and structure for your day reduces stress and allows you to approach tasks with a calmer mindset. Instead of feeling overwhelmed by multiple projects and looming deadlines, you can tackle them systematically.

3. Improve Decision-Making:

Time management enables you to allocate your resources effectively, making it easier to make informed decisions. By having a clear overview of your commitments, you can better determine whether to accept or decline new opportunities.

4. Maintain Work-Life Balance:

Entrepreneurship often demands long hours and intense dedication. However, effective time management can help you strike a balance between work and personal life. By optimizing your productivity, you can allocate time for self-care, family, and leisure activities.

Practical Techniques for Time Management

Now that we understand the significance of time management, let's explore some practical techniques that can help you master this skill:

1. Prioritize and Set Clear Goals:

Begin by identifying your most important tasks and goals. Prioritize them based on their impact on your business and the urgency of completion. Setting clear goals will provide you with a roadmap for your day and help you stay focused.

2. Plan and Organize:

Use a planner, digital calendar, or task management tool to schedule your activities and commitments. Break down larger tasks into smaller, manageable steps, and allocate time slots specifically for each task. This structured approach will increase your productivity and ensure that important tasks are not overlooked.

3. Eliminate Time Wasters:

Identify activities that consume significant amounts of time without contributing to your goals or productivity. It could be excessive social media usage, unnecessary meetings, or aimless web browsing. Minimize or eliminate these time wasters to reclaim lost hours in your day.

4. Delegate and Outsource:

Recognize that you cannot do everything on your own. Learn to delegate tasks that can be handled by others, allowing you to focus on higher-level responsibilities. Additionally, consider outsourcing tasks that are not within your expertise. This allows you to leverage external expertise and frees up your time for more valuable activities.

5. Utilize Technology and Tools:

Leverage technology and productivity tools to streamline your workflow. From project management software to automation tools, these resources can help simplify tasks, track progress, and enhance collaboration. Find tools that align with your specific needs and integrate them into your routine.

6. Embrace the Power of Saying 'No':

As entrepreneurs, we often feel obligated to say 'yes' to every opportunity that comes our way. However, this can lead to over-commitment and a scattered focus. Learn to say 'no' gracefully to activities that do not align with your goals or would stretch your resources too thin.

Conclusion

Effective time management sets the stage for success as an entrepreneur. It allows you to optimize your productivity, reduce stress, and maintain a healthy work-life balance. By implementing the techniques outlined in this first half of the chapter, you will be equipped to take charge of your time and make the most of each day. Stay tuned for the second part of this chapter, where we will delve deeper into additional strategies and tools to further enhance your time management skills. Keep reading to unlock the full potential of your entrepreneurial journey!

Developing Effective Habits for Time Management

Now that we have discussed some practical techniques for time management in the first half of this chapter, let's delve deeper into developing effective habits that will further enhance your ability to manage your time efficiently.

1. Embrace Time Blocking

Time blocking involves dividing your day into specific blocks of time dedicated to specific tasks or activities. This technique helps you allocate sufficient time for important tasks and ensures that you have dedicated periods of focused work. Instead of multitasking or constantly switching between tasks, time blocking allows you to give your full attention to one task at a time, leading to improved productivity and better quality work.

When implementing time blocking, it is essential to identify your most productive time of the day and assign your most important and challenging tasks to those periods. This way, you can leverage your peak energy and focus to accomplish crucial work. Additionally, be realistic about the time needed for each task and avoid overloading your schedule. Allow buffer time between blocks to accommodate unexpected interruptions or delays.

2. Practice the Pomodoro Technique

The Pomodoro Technique is a time management method developed by Francesco Cirillo. It involves working in short, focused bursts followed by brief breaks. The technique is named after the tomato-shaped kitchen timer used by Cirillo during his university days.

To practice the Pomodoro Technique, follow these steps:

- Set a timer for 25 minutes and fully commit to working on one task during that time. This is known as one Pomodoro.

- Once the timer goes off, take a short break of around 5 minutes. Use this time to stretch, hydrate, or clear your mind.

- After completing four Pomodoros (four consecutive 25-minute work periods), take a more extended break of 15-30 minutes. Use this break to recharge, engage in a quick physical activity, or engage in a mindful practice.

This technique helps you maintain focus and productivity by breaking your work into manageable, time-limited segments. It also prevents burnout by incorporating regular breaks, which can enhance creativity and problem-solving abilities. Experiment with different Pomodoro durations to find the ideal length for your work style and preferences.

3. Set Boundaries and Say No

As an entrepreneur, it's common to feel the pressure to say yes to every opportunity that comes your way. However, this can lead to overcommitment, burnout, and a lack of focus on your priorities. Learning to set boundaries and say no gracefully is essential for effective time management.

When considering new commitments or requests, evaluate whether they align with your goals, values, and available resources. If an opportunity or task does not fit within your overall plan, be confident in politely declining. Emphasize that your time and energy are precious resources that need to be allocated wisely. Remember, saying no to one thing allows you to say yes to what truly matters.

4. Practice Regular Review and Reflection

Taking the time to review and reflect on your time management practices is crucial for ongoing improvement. Set regular intervals to assess your productivity, identify areas of improvement, and make necessary adjustments. Consider scheduling weekly or monthly check-ins where you analyze how effectively you utilized your time and identify any patterns or habits that hindered your productivity.

During these reviews, ask yourself:

- Did I effectively prioritize and complete my most important tasks?

- Were there any time-wasting activities that can be eliminated?

- Did I delegate or outsource tasks appropriately?

- Did I adhere to my planned schedule and time blocks?

- Did I allocate enough time for rest and self-care?

By identifying areas of improvement and implementing necessary changes, you can continuously optimize your time management skills and increase your productivity.

5. Cultivate a Growth Mindset

Developing a growth mindset is crucial for embracing time management as an ongoing learning process. Embrace the idea that you can always improve your time management skills and adapt to new strategies as your business evolves. Celebrate successes and accomplishments, but also view setbacks or time management challenges as opportunities for growth and learning.

A growth mindset allows you to approach time management with curiosity, resilience, and a willingness to try new techniques. It helps you recognize that you have the ability to shape your destiny as an entrepreneur by consistently honing your time management skills.

In conclusion, mastering time management is a continuous journey that requires commitment, practice, and adaptability. By embracing time blocking, practicing the Pomodoro Technique, setting boundaries, engaging in regular review and reflection, and cultivating a growth mindset, you will develop effective habits that optimize your productivity and help you shape your destiny as an entrepreneur. Stay tuned for further chapters in this book, where we will explore additional strategies and tools to support your entrepreneurial journey. Remember, effective time management is the key to unlocking your full potential as an entrepreneur.

Chapter 6

Navigating Risk and Uncertainty

In the world of entrepreneurship, embarking on a new venture is like setting sail on unchartered waters. It is a thrilling journey filled with limitless possibilities, but it is also accompanied by the inevitable presence of risk and uncertainty. As aspiring entrepreneurs, early-stage entrepreneurs, or anyone with a mission mindset, it is crucial to understand the intricacies of evaluating and managing risks, making informed decisions, and embracing uncertainty.

Many avoid risk like the plague, fearing the potential failure and setbacks it may bring. However, it is important to recognize that risk is an inherent part of any entrepreneurial journey. The key lies in learning how to assess and manage risks effectively, rather than simply avoiding them altogether. By adopting a proactive approach towards risk, entrepreneurs can turn uncertainties into opportunities for growth and development.

The first step in navigating risk is to develop a keen ability to evaluate potential hazards and weigh

them against potential gains. Understanding the probability and potential impact of each risk allows entrepreneurs to make informed decisions. Proper risk assessment involves identifying and analyzing the various factors that could impact the success or failure of the venture. This includes analyzing market dynamics, competition, financial implications, and potential external threats. By conducting thorough research and considering multiple perspectives, entrepreneurs can better understand the risks they face and develop strategies to mitigate them.

Once the risks are identified, entrepreneurs must then develop effective risk management strategies. Risk management involves implementing plans and actions to minimize the impact of potential risks. This may involve diversifying resources, developing contingency plans, or seeking expert advice. For example, if the risk involves financial instability, entrepreneurs can consider establishing partnerships or securing alternative sources of funding to buffer themselves against potential downturns. Effective risk management not only protects entrepreneurs from potential setbacks but also builds resilience and adaptability within the venture.

Entrepreneurs must also navigate another challenging aspect of the entrepreneurial journey - uncertainty. Uncertainty arises from various sources, such as market fluctuations, changing consumer preferences, or technological advancements. While uncertainty can be intimidating, it can also be a catalyst for innovation and growth. Embracing uncertainty requires a mindset shift, turning the fear of the unknown into a mindset of curiosity and opportunity.

To embrace uncertainty, entrepreneurs must cultivate a learning mindset. This involves continuously seeking knowledge and staying abreast of industry trends. By understanding the evolving landscape, entrepreneurs can anticipate potential shifts and adapt their strategies accordingly. Additionally, fostering a culture of experimentation and iteration allows entrepreneurs to test new ideas, gather feedback, and make necessary adjustments. Embracing uncertainty requires a willingness to step outside of comfort zones and explore new possibilities.

However, uncertainty should not be confused with recklessness. While embracing uncertainty is essential, it is equally important to balance it with calculated decision-making. Successful entrepreneurs are those who can strike a delicate balance between taking calculated risks and making informed decisions. This requires gathering and analyzing relevant data, seeking expert advice when needed, and trusting one's intuition. It is the art of blending rational analysis with intuitive insights.

As entrepreneurs, we must remember that navigating risk and uncertainty is not a linear journey. **It is a continuous process of learning, adapting, and seizing opportunities.** The first half of this chapter has set the foundation for understanding the importance of evaluating and managing risks, making informed decisions, and embracing uncertainty. In the second half of this chapter, we will delve deeper into specific strategies and practical steps to effectively navigate these challenges. But for now, let us leave you with this thought: in the face of risk and uncertainty lies the potential for growth and success. Embrace the unknown, stay resilient, and continue on your mission mindset journey.In the second half of this chapter, we will delve deeper into specific strategies and practical steps to effectively navigate the challenges of risk and uncertainty. By equipping ourselves with these tools, we can foster a mission mindset that thrives in the face of adversity.

One crucial strategy for navigating risk and uncertainty is to cultivate a strong network of support and mentorship. **Surrounding yourself with like-minded individuals who have faced similar challenges can provide valuable insights and guidance.** Seek out mentors who have experience in your industry or have successfully navigated the entrepreneurial journey themselves. Their wisdom and perspective can help you make informed decisions and avoid potential pitfalls.

Another strategy is to **develop a mindset of resilience and adaptability.** In an ever-changing business landscape, being able to pivot and adapt to unexpected circumstances is crucial. Embrace failure as a learning opportunity and use setbacks as stepping stones towards growth. By maintaining a flexible mindset, you can turn obstacles into opportunities for innovation and improvement.

Furthermore, **effective communication and collaboration are essential for navigating uncertainty**. Building strong relationships with stakeholders, partners, and customers can help mitigate potential risks. By fostering open lines of communication, you can gather valuable feedback, identify blind spots, and adapt your strategies accordingly. Collaboration also allows you to leverage the expertise and resources of others, reducing the burden of uncertainty on your own shoulders.

In addition to these strategies, it is important to **continuously monitor and evaluate the risks you face.** While risk assessment is often done at the outset of a venture, it should be an ongoing process. Regularly reassess the potential risks and identify any new threats or opportunities that may arise. This will enable you to make proactive decisions and adjust your course as needed.

Another practical step in navigating risk and uncertainty is to **identify and mitigate potential financial risks.** Financial stability is crucial for the sustainability of any venture. Develop a robust financial plan that takes into account potential downturns, unexpected expenses, and market fluctuations. Diversify your revenue streams and explore alternative funding options to ensure you have a safety net in place.

Furthermore, **staying up to date with industry trends, technological advancements, and consumer preferences is vital for navigating uncertainty**. Continuously invest in your knowledge and skills through ongoing education, attending conferences, and networking events. By staying ahead of the curve, you can identify emerging opportunities and position your venture for success.

Lastly, **celebrating small victories and milestones along the way is essential for maintaining motivation and momentum.** Entrepreneurship is a challenging journey, and there will undoubtedly be setbacks and obstacles. By acknowledging and celebrating your wins, no matter how small, you can cultivate a positive mindset and fuel your drive to continue pushing forward.

To summarize, navigating risk and uncertainty requires a combination of strategies, mindset shifts, and practical steps. By cultivating a strong support network, embracing failure as a learning opportunity, fostering open communication and collaboration, continuously monitoring and evaluating risks, mitigating financial risks, staying informed about industry trends, and celebrating victories along the way, you can navigate the entrepreneurial journey with confidence and resilience.

Remember, the path to success is not without its challenges, but in the face of risk and uncertainty lies the potential for growth and success. Embrace the unknown, stay resilient, and continue on your mission mindset journey. With the right mindset, strategies, and actions, you can shape your destiny as an entrepreneur and achieve your goals.

~

Chapter 7

Building a Solid Network

I n a world increasingly driven by interconnectedness, the ability to forge strong and meaningful relationships is paramount for entrepreneurial success. Networking, defined as the act of making connections and building relationships with like-minded individuals, plays a pivotal role in shaping your destiny as an entrepreneur. It goes beyond simply collecting business cards or attending industry events; it is about fostering a sense of community, support, and collaboration. In this chapter, we will explore the importance of networking, building meaningful relationships, and leveraging connections for entrepreneurial success.

Networking has evolved from being a mere transactional process to a strategic tool that helps entrepreneurs expand their horizons and discover new opportunities. Regardless of whether you are a student, marketer, aspiring entrepreneur, early-stage entrepreneur, side hustler, career changer, personal development enthusiast, or a social and environmental change maker, networking presents a wealth of benefits.

For students and aspiring entrepreneurs, networking opens

41

doors to mentorship and guidance from experienced individuals who have already walked the path you aspire to take. It provides invaluable opportunities to learn from their successes and failures, helping you navigate the complex world of entrepreneurship with a clearer perspective. Moreover, networking allows you to tap into hidden job markets, gain access to internships, and unlock potential funding opportunities.

For marketers and early-stage entrepreneurs, networking acts as a catalyst for growth. By establishing connections with industry professionals and potential clients, you can leverage these relationships to amplify your business's reach and secure strategic partnerships. Collaborations forged through networking can lead to joint ventures, shared resources, and a broader customer base, propelling your venture towards success.

Side hustlers and career changers can also benefit significantly from networking. By connecting with individuals who have successfully transitioned careers or built successful side businesses, you can gain valuable insights and guidance. These interactions can help you lay the foundation for a successful side hustle or facilitate your transition into a completely new career path.

Personal development enthusiasts recognise networking as an opportunity for self-improvement and growth. Engaging with individuals who share your passion for personal development fosters a shared learning experience. Whether it is discovering new books, attending seminars, or participating in mastermind groups, networking offers a plethora of resources to enhance your personal growth journey.

In our ever-changing world, social and environmental issues have taken center stage. For social and environmental change makers, networking is an essential tool for creating a larger impact. It allows you to connect with like-minded individuals who share your passion for driving positive change. By establishing a strong network, you can collaborate on initiatives, pool resources, and amplify your collective voice, making a more significant difference in the world.

Now that we understand the diverse range of individuals who can benefit from networking, let's delve into the strategies for building a solid network. Over the years, entrepreneurs have developed various approaches to expand their connections, both in-person and online.

Firstly, attending industry events and conferences presents an opportunity to meet like-minded individuals face-to-face. These events often attract a diverse range of professionals, making them ideal platforms for building a network. Engaging in meaningful conversations, exchanging ideas, and showcasing your expertise can help forge valuable connections that go beyond the event itself.

Secondly, online networking platforms have gained significant traction in recent years. Platforms like LinkedIn serve as virtual hubs for professionals and entrepreneurs to connect, share insights, and collaborate. Utilize these platforms to build a strong online presence through thought leadership, engaging in relevant conversations, and actively seeking out connections aligned with your vision and goals.

Thirdly, consider joining industry-specific communities or groups. These online forums provide an avenue for networking within a niche. By joining conversations, offering expertise, and seeking advice, you can build meaningful relationships with individuals who understand your industry's intricacies and can offer valuable insights.

Lastly, don't underestimate the power of peer-to-peer networking. Engage with fellow entrepreneurs and professionals in your community or industry. Attend meetups, workshops, or even organize your own events. These interactions can lead to long-lasting relationships, shared learnings, and potentially even co-founded ventures.

As we conclude the first half of this chapter, we hope you have gained a deeper understanding of the importance of networking for entrepreneurial success. The benefits of networking are vast, regardless of your background or aspirations. In the second half of this chapter, we will explore impactful networking strategies and provide practical tips to leverage your connections effectively. So, stay tuned as we dive deeper into the world of networking and guide you on the path to building a solid network that will shape your destiny as an entrepreneur.In the second half of this chapter, we will delve deeper into the world of networking and provide you with practical tips to leverage your connections effectively. We will explore impactful networking strategies that can help you build a solid network, shaping your destiny as an entrepreneur.

One powerful networking strategy is to seek out mentorship and guidance from experienced individuals who have already walked the path you aspire to take. As a student or aspiring entrepreneur, connecting with mentors can provide invaluable opportunities to learn from their successes and failures. They can offer guidance in navigating the complex world of entrepreneurship with a clearer perspective. By leveraging their knowledge and expertise, you can gain practical insights that will propel your entrepreneurial journey forward.

For marketers and early-stage entrepreneurs, networking can act as a catalyst for growth. By establishing connections with industry professionals and potential clients, you can leverage these relationships to amplify your business's reach and secure strategic partnerships. Collaborations forged through networking can lead to joint ventures, shared resources, and a broader customer base, propelling your venture towards success.

Side hustlers and career changers can also benefit significantly from networking. By connecting with individuals who have successfully transitioned careers or built successful side businesses, you can gain valuable insights and guidance. These interactions can help you lay the foundation for a successful side hustle or facilitate your transition into a completely new career path. The knowledge and experience shared by these individuals can greatly contribute to your personal and professional development.

Personal development enthusiasts recognize networking as an opportunity for self-improvement and growth. Engaging with individuals who share your passion for personal development fosters a shared learning experience. Whether it is discovering new books, attending seminars, or participating in mastermind groups, networking offers a plethora of resources to enhance your personal growth journey. By connecting with like-minded individuals, you can expand your knowledge base and challenge yourself to reach new heights.

In our ever-changing world, social and environmental issues have taken center stage. For social and environmental change makers, networking is an essential tool for creating a larger impact. It allows you to connect with like-minded individuals who share your passion for driving positive change. By establishing a strong network, you can collaborate on initiatives, pool resources, and amplify your collective voice, making a more significant difference in the world.

Now that we understand the diverse range of individuals who can benefit from networking, let's explore some effective networking strategies.

Firstly, attending industry events and conferences presents an excellent opportunity to meet like-minded individuals face-to-face. These events often attract a diverse range of professionals, making them ideal platforms for building a network. Engaging in meaningful conversations, exchanging ideas, and showcasing your expertise can help forge valuable connections that go beyond the event itself.

Secondly, online networking platforms have gained significant traction in recent years. Platforms like LinkedIn serve as virtual hubs for professionals and entrepreneurs to connect, share insights, and collaborate. Utilize these platforms to build a strong online presence through thought leadership, engaging in relevant conversations, and actively seeking out connections aligned with your vision and goals.

Thirdly, consider joining industry-specific communities or groups. These online forums provide an avenue for networking within a niche. By joining conversations, offering expertise, and seeking advice, you can build meaningful relationships with individuals who understand your industry's intricacies and can offer valuable insights.

Lastly, don't underestimate the power of peer-to-peer networking. Engage with fellow entrepreneurs and professionals in your community or industry. Attend meetups, workshops, or even organize your own events. These interactions can lead to long-lasting relationships, shared learnings, and potentially even co-founded ventures.

While networking is a valuable tool, it's essential to approach it with authenticity and genuine interest in others. Building meaningful relationships takes time and effort, focusing not only on what you can gain from the connection but also on how you can contribute and add value to others' journeys.

In conclusion, networking is a powerful tool in shaping your destiny as an entrepreneur. By actively seeking connections and building relationships, you can open doors to mentorship, collaboration, and new opportunities. The benefits of networking are vast, regardless of your background or aspirations. It is a lifelong journey that requires continuous effort and nurturing. By incorporating these networking strategies and staying open to new connections, you can build a solid network that will support and guide you on your entrepreneurial path. So, go out there, connect, inspire, and shape your destiny as an entrepreneur.

Chapter 8

Defining Your Target Market

I n the world of entrepreneurship, understanding your target market is paramount to success. As an aspiring entrepreneur, marketer, or even a side hustler, identifying and truly comprehending your target market is the foundation upon which you build your business. It is the key that unlocks the doors to exponential growth and sustains your venture in the long run. In this chapter, we will delve deep into the art of defining your target market, exploring the intricacies and strategies that will set you apart from the competition.

Actionable steps to identify your target market

To embark on this journey of defining your target market, you must first recognize the importance of thorough research. Understanding your audience, their needs, desires, pain points, and aspirations is a fundamental step toward crafting effective marketing strategies. Market research allows you to gain valuable insights into your target market, ensuring that you offer the right product or service to the right people at the right time.

One effective way to begin your research is by conducting surveys, interviews, or focus groups. These methods enable you to directly interact with potential customers, collecting valuable data and understanding their perspectives. By asking relevant questions, you can uncover the challenges they face, what motivates their purchase decisions, and the solutions they seek. This invaluable data provides a solid foundation for your marketing endeavors.

Additionally, analyzing market trends, competitor strategies, and industry reports can provide a broader view of your target market. Stay updated with the latest market developments, emerging technologies, and consumer preferences. Utilize online resources, industry publications, and social media platforms to gather information and identify patterns that influence your target market.

While conducting research, it's crucial to segment your target market. This involves dividing your potential customers into distinct groups based on shared characteristics, interests, demographics, or behavior. By segmenting your market, you can create tailored marketing messages and campaigns that resonate with specific segments of your audience. This personalized approach enhances engagement and increases the likelihood of converting potential customers into loyal advocates of your brand.

Once you have defined your target segments, it's time to develop buyer personas. Buyer personas are fictional representations of your ideal customers, crafted using a combination of research, insights, and imagination. With buyer personas, you can humanize your target market, creating a deeper understanding of their goals, motivations, and pain points. This understanding enables you to craft marketing messages that connect with your audience on a personal level, driving meaningful interactions and building long-lasting relationships.

As you delve deeper into understanding your target market, remember that the journey doesn't end with defining their needs and desires. An effective entrepreneur goes beyond simply understanding; they anticipate and adapt to the evolving landscape. Keep a keen eye on emerging trends, disruptive technologies, and changing consumer behaviors. What may be relevant today could be outdated tomorrow. Stay agile and adapt your strategies accordingly to maintain a competitive edge.

In conclusion, the process of defining your target market is a multifaceted one. It requires diligent research, segmentation, and the development of buyer personas. Understanding your audience on a deeper level enables you to tailor your marketing strategies, capture their attention, and meet their needs effectively. However, this is only the first half of our exploration into this critical topic. Stay tuned for the second half of this chapter where we will discuss effective marketing strategies and tactics to reach and engage your target market. Get ready to take your entrepreneurial journey to the next level and unlock the keys to success.

Developing effective marketing strategies to reach your target market

Once you have a clear understanding of your target market and have defined their needs and desires, it's time to develop **actionable marketing strategies** that will resonate with them. Effective marketing is not a one-size-fits-all approach, as different target segments may require different tactics to capture their attention. Let's explore some key strategies that will help you engage and connect with your target market.

1. Craft a compelling value proposition: Your value

proposition is the unique selling point of your product or service that sets you apart from competitors. It should clearly communicate the value you offer to your target market and how you solve their pain points. By focusing on the unique benefits and outcomes, you can effectively capture their attention and address their needs.

2. Utilize social media platforms: In today's digital age, social media has become one of the most powerful marketing tools. Identify the social media platforms where your target market spends their time and develop a strong presence on those platforms. Share engaging content, interact with your audience, and leverage targeted advertisements to reach a wider audience.

3. Create compelling content: Content marketing is an effective way to engage your target market and establish yourself as a thought leader in your industry. Develop high-quality content that educates, entertains, or inspires your audience. This could include blog posts, videos, podcasts, or social media posts that address their pain points and provide valuable insights. By consistently delivering valuable content, you can build trust and credibility with your target market.

4. Implement search engine optimization (SEO) techniques: When your target market is searching for products or services online, you want your business to be easily discoverable. By optimizing your website and content for search engines, you can improve your visibility in search results. Conduct keyword research to identify the terms and phrases your target market is using and incorporate them strategically in your website copy, blog posts, and meta descriptions.

5. Leverage influencer marketing: Influencers have a strong following and can significantly impact the purchasing decisions of their audience. Identify influencers who align with your brand and target market, and collaborate with them to promote your product or service. Their endorsement can increase your visibility and credibility among your target market.

6. Implement email marketing campaigns: Email marketing allows you to nurture relationships with your target market and stay top-of-mind. Develop a compelling email marketing strategy that provides value to your subscribers through personalized content, exclusive offers, and updates on new products or services. By segmenting your email list based on the interests and preferences of your target market, you can deliver relevant content that resonates with them.

7. Monitor and analyze your marketing efforts: To ensure the effectiveness of your marketing strategies, it's important to track and analyze your results. Utilize analytics tools to measure the performance of your campaigns, such as website traffic, conversion rates, and customer engagement. This data will provide valuable insights into what is working and what needs improvement, allowing you to refine your strategies for optimal results.

As an entrepreneur, it's important to continually adapt and refine your marketing strategies to meet the changing needs and preferences of your target market. Stay informed about the latest industry trends and consumer behaviors. Regularly reassess your target market and adjust your strategies accordingly to maintain a competitive edge in the market.

In conclusion, understanding and defining your target market is the first step towards building a successful entrepreneurial venture. By conducting thorough research, segmenting your market, and developing buyer personas, you gain a deeper understanding of your audience's needs and desires. With this knowledge, you can craft effective marketing strategies that resonate with your target market, driving meaningful interactions and building long-lasting relationships. By implementing key marketing strategies like developing a compelling value proposition, utilizing social media, creating compelling content, implementing SEO techniques, leveraging influencer marketing, conducting email marketing campaigns, and monitoring your efforts, you can effectively reach and engage your target market. Now, armed with these strategies, you are ready to take your entrepreneurial journey to the next level and shape your destiny as an entrepreneur.

Chapter 9

Creating a Compelling Brand

When it comes to establishing a successful business, having a compelling brand is a crucial element. Your brand is not just a name or a logo; it represents the entire identity of your venture. It is what sets you apart from your competitors and connects you with your target audience. In this chapter, we will explore the elements of a strong brand identity and guide you on how to effectively communicate your brand's value to your intended market.

A strong brand identity consists of various components that work together harmoniously to create a unique and memorable impression. One of the key elements is establishing a clear brand purpose. Your purpose defines why your business exists and the impact you aim to make. It is the driving force behind your entrepreneurial journey and should align with your personal values. By identifying your purpose, you can build a brand that resonates deeply with both you and your customers.

Another vital aspect of building a compelling brand is crafting your **brand's mission statement**. This statement outlines your long-term objectives and serves as a guiding principle for your business decisions. A compelling mission statement not only clarifies your purpose but also communicates your brand's unique value proposition. It should inspire your target audience and evoke emotions that foster a sense of loyalty and connection.

In addition to purpose and a mission statement, your brand needs a **distinct personality**. Your brand's personality determines how it communicates and interacts with your audience. Is your brand playful and lighthearted or serious and professional? Knowing your brand's personality helps you choose the appropriate tone and style for your communication, ensuring consistency across all touchpoints.

Furthermore, **visuals** play a significant role in establishing a strong brand identity. A visually appealing and consistent brand design is a powerful tool for creating recognition and fostering brand loyalty. This includes well-designed logos, color schemes, typography, and imagery that reflect your brand's essence. These visual elements should resonate with your target audience and evoke emotions that align with your brand's values.

Effective communication is vital for conveying your brand's value to your audience. To achieve this, you need to understand your target market inside out. Conduct thorough market research to identify the demographics, psychographics, and preferences of your potential customers. This knowledge will enable you to tailor your messaging to resonate with your audience's needs and desires.

Storytelling is another powerful tool for effective brand communication. Humans are wired to connect with stories, making them an ideal medium for conveying your brand's purpose and values. Craft a compelling narrative that reflects your brand's journey and showcases the impact you aspire to make. Tell stories that resonate with your audience's aspirations, emotions, and desires, as this will help forge a strong connection between your brand and your target market.

Now that we have explored the elements of a strong brand identity, it's time to delve into the **art of effective communication**. To effectively communicate your brand's value, you must craft compelling messages that address your audience's pain points and demonstrate how your product or service can solve their problems. Highlight the unique benefits and features that set you apart from your competitors, and establish yourself as a trusted authority in your industry.

Through various channels, such as social media, websites, and content marketing, you can engage with your audience and reinforce your brand's value proposition. Consistent and strategic communication builds brand awareness and fosters a loyal customer base. Utilize social media platforms, create engaging content, and embrace storytelling to keep your audience captivated.

As you immerse yourself in the process of creating a compelling brand, remember that it is an ongoing journey. The first half of this chapter has provided you with a solid foundation to begin shaping your brand identity and effectively communicating your brand's value. The second half, which will be unveiled later, will delve further into the intricacies of brand development and guide you on the implementation of your brand strategy. Whether you are a student, marketer, aspiring entrepreneur, or early-stage entrepreneur, mastering the art of creating a compelling brand is essential for your success in the business world. So, stay tuned for the next part, where we will explore the practical steps you can take to bring your brand to life and captivate your target audience.In the first half of this chapter, we laid the groundwork for creating a compelling brand identity and effectively communicating your brand's value to your target audience. Now, let's delve even deeper into the intricacies of brand development and explore the practical steps you can take to bring your brand to life and captivate your audience.

One crucial aspect of brand development is defining your brand's positioning. Positioning refers to how you want your brand to be perceived in the marketplace compared to your competitors. To establish a strong position, you need to identify your **unique selling proposition (USP)** and communicate it clearly to your audience.

Your USP is the specific feature or benefit that sets your product or service apart from others in the market. It highlights the value you offer and the problems you solve for your customers. Take the time to identify your USP by conducting market research, analyzing your competitors, and understanding the needs and desires of your target audience. Once you've identified your USP, craft a clear and concise message that articulates it effectively.

Once you have defined your positioning and USP, it's essential to develop a comprehensive brand strategy to guide your business decisions and actions. A brand strategy is a roadmap that outlines how you will achieve your branding goals and connect with your audience. It includes elements such as your brand's vision, mission, values, and personality.

Your brand's vision is a long-term aspiration that describes the future state you want your brand to achieve. It sets the direction and goals for your brand and provides a sense of purpose and direction. Your mission, on the other hand, outlines the practical steps you will take to fulfill your vision. It aligns with your brand's purpose and communicates the value you bring to your customers. Your values are the guiding principles that dictate how you do business and the beliefs that underpin your brand's actions.

With your brand strategy in place, it's time to bring your brand to life visually. Visual branding elements, such as your logo, color scheme, typography, and imagery, play a significant role in creating a strong brand identity. Ensure that your visual elements are consistent and aligned with your brand's personality, values, and target audience.

When designing your logo, consider both aesthetics and symbolism. Your logo should be visually appealing while also embodying the essence of your brand and conveying a clear message. Colors can evoke emotions and have specific associations, so choose a color palette that aligns with your brand's personality and resonates with your target audience. Typography also contributes to your brand's visual identity by conveying a specific tone and style. Select fonts that are legible, reflect your brand's personality, and enhance the overall design. Additionally, carefully curate your imagery to ensure it aligns with your brand's values, resonates with your target audience, and supports your messaging.

Once you have developed your visual branding elements, it's crucial to establish consistency across all touchpoints. Consistency helps your audience recognize and remember your brand, creating a sense of familiarity and trust. Make sure your visual branding is consistently applied on your website, social media platforms, marketing materials, and any other customer-facing touchpoints.

In addition to visual branding, effective communication through various channels is vital for building brand awareness and connecting with your audience. Social media platforms provide an excellent opportunity to engage with your target audience, share valuable content, and build relationships. Utilize social media to tell your brand's story, showcase your expertise, and create a sense of community around your brand. Remember to tailor your messaging to resonate with your audience's needs and desires, maintaining a consistent tone and style reflective of your brand's personality.

Another channel for effective communication is content marketing. By creating high-quality and valuable content, such as blog posts, videos, or podcasts, you can establish yourself as an industry expert and provide genuine value to your audience. Focus on addressing your audience's pain points, answering their questions, and offering actionable insights. This not only builds trust and credibility but also positions your brand as a go-to resource in your industry.

Lastly, consider the **power of storytelling** in your brand communication. Humans are naturally drawn to stories, and storytelling is an effective tool to forge a deep connection between your brand and your target market. Craft compelling narratives that align with your brand's purpose, values, and the aspirations of your audience. Use storytelling to communicate the impact you want to make and to create an emotional bond with your customers.

As we conclude this chapter on creating a compelling brand, it's important to remember that brand development is an ongoing process. Continually refine and evolve your brand as your business grows and adapts to changing market conditions. Regularly evaluate your brand's performance, gather feedback from your customers, and make necessary adjustments to stay relevant and resonant.

Whether you are a student, marketer, aspiring entrepreneur, or an individual seeking personal development, mastering the art of creating a compelling brand is essential for success in today's business world. By understanding the elements of a strong brand identity, knowing how to effectively communicate your brand's value, and implementing a comprehensive brand strategy, you can build a brand that stands out from the competition and resonates deeply with your target audience.

Now armed with the knowledge and practical steps outlined in this chapter, it's time to embark on your brand development journey and shape your destiny as an entrepreneur. Let your brand's uniqueness shine, captivate your audience, and make a lasting impact on the world.

~

Chapter 10

Crafting an Irresistible Value Proposition

Discover the importance of developing a unique and compelling value proposition that differentiates your business in the market.

In today's highly competitive business landscape, finding ways to stand out and capture the attention of your target audience is crucial. As an entrepreneur, you need to craft a value proposition that not only sets your business apart from the competition but also resonates with your customers and drives them to choose your products or services. A well-developed value proposition can be the key to unlocking your business's success.

Understanding Value Proposition

But what exactly is a value proposition? In simple terms, it is a concise statement that conveys the unique benefits customers can expect from your offerings and how they are better than what competitors provide. It is a clear articulation of the value you deliver to your customers and the problems you help them solve. A compelling value proposition ensures that your target audience understands why they should choose your business over others and how it addresses their specific pain points.

To craft an irresistible value proposition, you must first deeply understand your target market and their needs. Investing time and effort in market research allows you to gain valuable insights into your customers' desires, pain points, and motivations. By understanding their deepest anxieties, aspirations, and goals, you can tailor your value proposition to speak directly to them.

Next, you need to analyze your competition. What are they offering? How do they position themselves in the market? Identifying gaps or weaknesses in their value propositions will help you identify opportunities to differentiate your business. By offering something unique and valuable that competitors don't, you can carve out a niche for yourself and attract customers who resonate with your approach.

Once you have a clear understanding of your target audience and competitive landscape, it's time to start crafting your unique value proposition. Start by defining the specific benefits your products or services offer. What problems do you solve? How do you make your customers' lives easier, better, or more enjoyable? Focus on the tangible outcomes they can expect from choosing your business.

To make your value proposition more compelling, consider incorporating elements that differentiate you further. Is there a specific feature or attribute of your products or services that sets you apart? Is there a unique approach or methodology you employ? By highlighting these distinct advantages, you create a sense of exclusivity and reinforce the value your business provides.

Remember to keep your value proposition clear, concise, and easily understandable. Avoid jargon or complex language that might confuse or alienate your audience. People need to grasp your value proposition quickly, so they can make an informed decision about whether to choose your business or look elsewhere.

Another essential aspect of crafting an irresistible value proposition is ensuring that it resonates emotionally with your audience. People make buying decisions based on emotions, then rationalize them with logical reasons. By tapping into your customers' emotions, you can create a strong bond and foster loyalty.

Consider how your value proposition can address your customers' emotional needs, such as belonging, accomplishment, or security. How can your offerings make them feel more confident, empowered, or fulfilled? By aligning your value proposition with these emotional drivers, you can create a strong connection that goes beyond mere product features.

Crafting an irresistible value proposition is an ongoing process. Refining and optimizing it should be a continuous effort as you learn more about your customers and marketplace dynamics. Keep an eye on industry trends, listen to customer feedback, and make adjustments accordingly. Remember, your value proposition should evolve alongside your business to maintain its relevance and effectiveness.

In the second half of this chapter, we will delve deeper into strategies and techniques to make your value proposition truly stand out. From leveraging storytelling to incorporating social proof and customer testimonials, we will explore how to elevate your value proposition to new heights.

Stay tuned for the next section, where we will provide you with actionable insights and practical tips to take your value proposition from good to extraordinary. We will unlock the secrets to capturing your audience's attention, igniting their curiosity, and leaving an indelible mark in their minds.

Exciting times lie ahead. Get ready to embark on a value proposition journey that will transform your business and set you on a path to success. Step into the world of mastering the art of crafting an irresistible value proposition in the next section.

Crafting an Irresistible Value Proposition

In the previous section, we discussed the importance of understanding your target market and analyzing your competition to create a compelling value proposition. Now, let's delve deeper into strategies and techniques that will elevate your value proposition to new heights.

Storytelling is a powerful tool for connecting with your audience on an emotional level. By incorporating storytelling into your value proposition, you can engage your customers and bring your brand to life. A story has the ability to evoke emotions, capture attention, and create a memorable experience. Consider integrating narratives that depict how your products or services have positively impacted customers' lives. Share success stories, testimonials, and case studies that illustrate the transformation your offerings can bring. When you can relate to your audience's emotions through storytelling, you create a lasting impression, building trust and loyalty.

Another effective way to enhance your value proposition is by incorporating social proof. People are more likely to trust a product or service if they see others giving it positive feedback. Incorporating testimonials from satisfied customers, displaying ratings and reviews, and showcasing partnerships or endorsements all contribute to building credibility and trust. Social proof acts as evidence that your offering delivers on its promises. When potential customers see that others have had positive experiences with your brand, it creates a sense of confidence and encourages them to choose your business.

In addition to **social proof**, incorporating **customer**

testimonials can be a valuable tool in strengthening your value proposition. Testimonials provide real-life examples of how your offerings have solved problems or fulfilled needs. Highlight specific success stories, outcomes, and the benefits customers have experienced. Use quotes or anecdotes to capture the essence of their satisfaction. To make testimonials even more compelling, include identifiable details such as names, photos, or even videos of your satisfied customers. The more relatable and genuine the testimonials, the stronger the impact on your target audience.

To make your value proposition truly extraordinary, consider incorporating a unique and **memorable visual element.** A well-designed logo or visual representation can leave a lasting impression on your audience and help differentiate your brand from competitors. Aim for a visual identity that aligns with your value proposition and resonates with your target market. Whether sleek and modern, or warm and playful, your visual identity should evoke the emotions and qualities you want associated with your brand. Visual branding can elevate your value proposition by conveying a sense of professionalism, authenticity, and cohesion.

Remember that an irresistible value proposition should always be centered around addressing your customers' pain points and desires. Continuously listening to customer feedback is vital for refining and optimizing your value proposition. Solicit feedback through surveys, focus groups, or social media platforms to gain insights into your customers' evolving needs and expectations. Regularly revisit and adapt your value proposition based on these learnings to ensure its relevance and effectiveness.

Stay up-to-date with industry trends and monitor your competition to identify any gaps or opportunities that would allow you to differentiate your business further. By staying ahead of the curve, you can proactively adjust your value proposition to meet emerging customer needs or to capitalize on market trends. This agility and adaptability will enable you to remain competitive and relevant in a constantly evolving business landscape.

In conclusion, crafting an irresistible value proposition requires a deep understanding of your target market, competitive analysis, and ongoing optimization. By incorporating storytelling, social proof, customer testimonials, and visual elements into your value proposition, you can create a powerful message that captivates your audience. Emphasize the unique benefits your offerings provide, address your customers' emotional needs, and continually refine your value proposition to stay ahead of the game.

Now armed with these insights and practical tips, it's time for you to embark on your own value proposition journey. Tap into the passions and aspirations of your target audience, express your brand's unique qualities, and confidently position yourself in the market. By mastering the art of crafting an irresistible value proposition, you will unlock the potential to shape your destiny as an entrepreneur and create a lasting impact on the world. Best of luck!

Chapter 11

Building a Sustainable Business Model

As an aspiring entrepreneur, building a sustainable and profitable venture should be at the forefront of your mind. In today's competitive business landscape, it is essential to explore various business models, understand their strengths and weaknesses, and strategically craft a model that aligns with your vision and goals. So, let's dive into the world of business models and discover the key factors to create a sustainable business.

Various Business Models

When it comes to business models, there is no one-size-fits-all solution. Each industry, market, and company is unique, requiring careful consideration and analysis. By understanding different business models, you can identify the right approach for your venture and make informed decisions that drive long-term success.

1. Traditional Business Model:

The traditional business model is a common starting point for many entrepreneurs. It involves identifying a market need and creating a product or service to fulfill that need. This model follows a straightforward approach of creating value, delivering it to customers, and generating revenue. It typically involves a one-time purchase and transactional relationships with customers.

While this model has stood the test of time, it can have limitations. In today's fast-paced world, customer preferences are constantly evolving, and businesses need to adapt to stay relevant. Furthermore, solely relying on one-time transactions may result in inconsistent revenue streams, making it challenging to sustain profitability in the long run.

2. Subscription-Based Model:

The subscription-based model has gained significant popularity in recent years due to its ability to provide consistent revenue streams. Instead of one-time purchases, customers pay a recurring fee to access the product or service. This model fosters ongoing relationships with customers, allowing businesses to focus on customer retention and experience.

For aspiring entrepreneurs, the subscription-based model provides stability and predictability. By continuously delivering value and maintaining customer satisfaction, businesses can establish a loyal customer base that generates recurring revenue. Additionally, this model often offers opportunities for upselling and cross-selling, further enhancing profitability.

3. Freemium Model:

In today's digital age, the freemium model has become pervasive, especially in software and online services industries. This model offers a basic version of the product or service for free, enticing customers to upgrade to a premium version with additional features and benefits.

The freemium model leverages the power of the "free" concept to attract a large user base. By offering a valuable product or service upfront, businesses can build brand awareness, establish trust, and drive customer acquisition. Once users experience the value provided by the free version, they are more likely to convert into paying customers for the premium offerings.

4. Marketplace Model:

Marketplace models, such as Airbnb and Uber, have disrupted traditional industries and revolutionized the way we consume goods and services. These platforms connect buyers and sellers, creating a network effect where the value of the platform increases with the number of participants.

For aspiring entrepreneurs, the marketplace model offers immense opportunities for growth and scalability. By effectively matching buyers and sellers, businesses can facilitate transactions and generate revenue through commissions or fees. However, building a marketplace requires careful consideration of factors like supply and demand dynamics, trust and safety, and fostering a vibrant community.

5. Social Impact Model:

In recent years, there has been a growing emphasis on businesses that incorporate social and environmental objectives into their operations. Social impact models aim to generate both financial returns and positive societal outcomes. These models often involve addressing social or environmental challenges while leveraging business strategies to create sustainable solutions.

For individuals passionate about making a difference, the social impact model provides a powerful framework to drive positive change. By aligning your business with a social mission, you can attract like-minded customers, investors, and partners who value the impact you create. However, balancing the financial sustainability of the venture while achieving social impact requires thoughtful planning and execution.

To summarise, exploring and understanding different business models is crucial in shaping your destiny as an entrepreneur. By identifying the strengths and weaknesses of various models, you can develop a sustainable and profitable venture that stands the test of time. In the second half of this chapter, we will delve deeper into refining your chosen business model and exploring strategies to ensure long-term success. So stay tuned for the exciting continuation of this chapter!

Now that you have explored various business models and gained a deeper understanding of their strengths and weaknesses, it's time to delve deeper into refining your chosen business model and exploring strategies to ensure long-term success. In the second half of this chapter, we will discuss key considerations and practical steps to build a sustainable business model that aligns with your vision and goals.

Key considerations

One crucial aspect of building a sustainable business model is identifying your target market and understanding their needs and preferences. Conducting market research and gathering customer insights will provide valuable information that can shape your product or service offerings. By truly understanding your target market, you can tailor your business model to meet their specific needs, which will increase the chances of success and sustainability.

Furthermore, it is essential to emphasize the importance of differentiation. In today's competitive business landscape, standing out from the crowd is crucial for sustainable success. Your business model should include unique value propositions that set you apart from competitors. Whether it's through superior customer service, innovative features, or a differentiated pricing structure, find ways to provide value that is difficult for others to replicate.

Another critical aspect to consider when building a sustainable business model is scalability. While starting small can be a wise approach, it is essential to have a clear plan for growth and expansion. Consider how your business can scale without compromising its core values or quality. This may involve exploring opportunities for partnerships, franchising, or utilizing technology to automate processes and increase efficiency. The ability to scale will not only contribute to your long-term profitability but also attract potential investors and stakeholders.

Moreover, a critical factor in building a sustainable business model is financial planning and management. By carefully monitoring and managing your finances, you can ensure the profitability and longevity of your venture. Develop a comprehensive financial strategy that includes accurate forecasting, budgeting, and monitoring your key performance indicators (KPIs). Regularly assess your business's financial health and make adjustments as needed to maintain stability and sustainability.

Additionally, leveraging technology can play a significant role in building a sustainable business model. In today's digital age, technology has become an invaluable tool for entrepreneurs. It can streamline processes, enhance customer experiences, and provide insights for data-driven decision-making. Consider how you can integrate technology into your business model, whether through developing an online presence, implementing automation software, or utilizing data analytics to optimize operations.

Another aspect to consider for long-term sustainability is building strong relationships with your customers. Customer retention should be a primary focus, as it is often more cost-effective to retain existing customers than acquire new ones. Implement strategies to continuously engage with your customers, gather feedback, and provide ongoing value. Personalize your interactions and offer exceptional customer service to foster loyalty and create brand advocates who will not only continue to support your business but also recommend it to others.

Furthermore, as an entrepreneur, it is crucial to continuously adapt and evolve your business model. The business landscape is constantly changing, and what works today may not work tomorrow. Stay informed about industry trends, emerging technologies, and shifts in customer preferences. Regularly evaluate and reassess your business model to ensure it remains aligned with the ever-evolving market dynamics. Be open to making adjustments and pivoting your strategy whenever necessary.

Finally, always remember the importance of maintaining a mission-driven mindset. As an entrepreneur, having a purpose beyond profit is crucial for long-term success and impact. Consider how you can incorporate social and environmental responsibility into your business model. By aligning your business with a social mission, you can attract like-minded customers, partners, and investors who value the positive impact you create.

In conclusion, building a sustainable business model requires careful consideration and planning. By focusing on understanding your target market, differentiating your offerings, and emphasizing scalability, financial management, technology integration, customer relationships, adaptability, and a mission-driven mindset, you can create a venture that stands the test of time. The key is to continually evaluate and refine your business model as you navigate the ever-changing business landscape. Remember, building a sustainable business model is a journey, and by equipping yourself with the right knowledge and mindset, you can shape your destiny as a successful entrepreneur.

⌒

Chapter 12

Leveraging Technology and Innovation

Technological advancements have always played a significant role in shaping the entrepreneurial land-scape. Innovations in technology have not only transformed industries but have also opened countless doors of opportunity for those willing to embrace them. In this chapter, we will explore the exciting realm of technology and how it can be leveraged to drive growth, streamline processes, and ultimately help entrepreneurs stay ahead in the ever-evolving business world.

1. Embracing Technological Disruption

In today's fast-paced world, it's crucial for entrepreneurs to recognize the transformative power of technology. From artificial intelligence and machine learning to blockchain and augmented reality, disruptive technologies are revolutionizing industries across the board. Embracing these advancements is no longer a choice but a necessity for success. Entrepreneurs need to have a curious and open mindset that welcomes change and actively seeks out opportunities to harness these technologies to their advantage.

2. Driving Growth Through Digital Transformation

Digital transformation has become a buzzword, but its impact on entrepreneurial ventures cannot be overstated. By leveraging technology, business owners can propel their organizations forward, reach wider audiences, and tap into new markets. From e-commerce platforms and digital marketing strategies to data analytics and customer relationship management, digital tools have become indispensable in driving growth. Entrepreneurs must adapt their strategies to incorporate digital transformation effectively, ensuring they ride the wave of technological advancements instead of being left behind.

3. Streamlining Processes for Efficiency

One of the most significant advantages of technology lies in its ability to streamline processes. Automation, for instance, can optimize repetitive tasks, freeing up valuable time and resources for entrepreneurs to focus on core business activities. By leveraging workflow management systems, cloud computing, and project management tools, entrepreneurs gain a competitive edge through enhanced productivity and operational efficiency. It is essential to identify areas within your business that can benefit from technological solutions and implement them strategically for maximum impact.

4. The Collaborative Potential of Technology

Technology has also revolutionized collaboration, breaking down barriers of time and distance. Entrepreneurs can now connect and collaborate with individuals across the globe, expanding their networks and accessing diverse skill sets. Virtual meetings, online project management platforms, and shared document repositories provide opportunities for entrepreneurs to tap into a global talent pool and establish partnerships that were previously unimaginable. By leveraging technology, entrepreneurs can build powerful ecosystems that boost creativity, innovation, and ultimately accelerate business growth.

5. Staying Ahead: The Need for Continuous Learning

In today's rapidly changing technological landscape, maintaining a competitive edge requires a commitment to constant learning. Entrepreneurs need to embrace a growth mindset and actively seek out knowledge about emerging technologies and industry trends. Continuous learning should be ingrained in an entrepreneur's DNA, allowing them to adapt swiftly and make informed decisions. Engaging in online courses, attending industry conferences, and joining entrepreneurial communities are all ways to stay attuned to technological advancements and position oneself at the forefront of innovation.

By effectively leveraging technology and innovation, entrepreneurs can march towards success in an ever-evolving business landscape. The possibilities are limitless, and the only boundaries are the ones we impose upon ourselves. In the second half of this chapter, we will delve deeper into specific technologies and strategies that can empower entrepreneurs on their mission to shape their destiny. Stay tuned as we explore the exciting and transformative potential waiting to be unlocked.

6. Maximizing Data and Analytics Insights

In the rapidly evolving entrepreneurial landscape, data has become a critical asset for businesses of all sizes. By harnessing the power of data and leveraging advanced analytics tools, entrepreneurs can gain valuable insights into their customers, markets, and overall business performance. Understanding how to effectively collect, analyze, and act upon data can provide a significant competitive advantage.

With the rise of big data, entrepreneurs have the opportunity to tap into a wealth of information that can drive decision-making and strategy development. By utilizing data analytics tools, entrepreneurs can identify patterns, trends, and correlations that may not be immediately apparent. This allows for informed decision-making and the ability to spot opportunities or potential challenges well in advance.

From customer behavior and preferences to market trends and competitor analysis, data provides entrepreneurs with a comprehensive understanding of the ecosystem in which they operate. This knowledge can inform product development, marketing campaigns, and overall business strategies, ultimately contributing to growth and success.

Furthermore, data-driven decision-making enables entrepreneurs to measure and evaluate the effectiveness of their initiatives, ensuring that resources are allocated efficiently and effectively. By continuously monitoring and analyzing key performance indicators (KPIs), entrepreneurs can make data-backed adjustments to their strategies as needed, mitigating risks and capturing opportunities.

It's crucial for entrepreneurs to invest in building the necessary infrastructure and capabilities to collect, store, and analyze data effectively. This may involve implementing data management systems and hiring or partnering with data experts who can navigate the complexities of extracting insights from raw data. By maximizing the potential of data and analytics, entrepreneurs can make informed decisions that can shape their destiny and propel their businesses forward.

7. Harnessing the Power of Artificial Intelligence

Artificial intelligence (AI) has become a game-changer for entrepreneurs, enabling them to automate processes, improve customer experiences, and gain a competitive edge. AI-powered chatbots, for example, can handle customer inquiries, providing immediate assistance and freeing up human resources for more complex tasks. Recommendation algorithms can analyze customer data, offering personalized suggestions and improving customer satisfaction.

Entrepreneurs can also leverage AI to enhance their marketing efforts. By utilizing machine learning algorithms, they can better understand their target audience, optimize ad campaigns, and deliver personalized content to attract and engage customers. AI can analyze vast amounts of data and generate actionable insights, allowing businesses to tailor their offerings and messaging accordingly.

Moreover, AI can assist entrepreneurs in identifying patterns and anomalies in their operational data, helping them identify areas where they can streamline processes, reduce costs, and improve efficiency. By automating mundane tasks and utilizing predictive analytics, entrepreneurs can focus on high-value activities that drive growth and innovation.

For aspiring entrepreneurs and early-stage businesses, AI can level the playing field by providing access to tools and technologies that were previously only available to large corporations. Cloud-based AI solutions are becoming more affordable and accessible, allowing entrepreneurs to integrate AI into their operations without substantial upfront investments.

To leverage the power of AI effectively, entrepreneurs should stay informed about recent advancements in AI technologies, and consider exploring partnerships or collaborations with AI startups or experts. By embracing AI and its capabilities, entrepreneurs can automate, optimize, and outperform in their respective industries, ultimately shaping their destiny in the ever-evolving entrepreneurial landscape.

8. Rethinking Cybersecurity in the Digital Age

As entrepreneurs embrace technology and digital transformation, it's crucial to prioritize cybersecurity to safeguard their businesses and their customers' trust. Cyber threats are ever-evolving, and entrepreneurs must remain vigilant to protect their sensitive data, systems, and networks from malicious attacks.

Implementing robust cybersecurity measures should be a top priority for entrepreneurs, regardless of the size or stage of their ventures. This includes securing networks, implementing encryption protocols, regularly updating software, and training employees on best cybersecurity practices.

Entrepreneurs should also be proactive in assessing and managing risks associated with data breaches or cyber-attacks. This involves conducting regular audits, penetration testing, and establishing incident response plans. Seeking the expertise of cybersecurity professionals or engaging with managed security service providers can also provide additional layers of protection.

Furthermore, entrepreneurs must prioritize user privacy and

data protection. This involves transparency in data collection and use, obtaining appropriate consent, and ensuring compliance with relevant regulations such as the General Data Protection Regulation (GDPR). By prioritizing data privacy, entrepreneurs can build trust with their customers and differentiate themselves in a crowded market.

9. Navigating Emerging Technologies and the Future Landscape

The entrepreneurial landscape will continue to evolve with the emergence of new and disruptive technologies. To shape their destiny, entrepreneurs must stay attuned to these emerging technologies and anticipate their impact on industries.

Emerging technologies such as the Internet of Things (IoT), virtual reality (VR), and 5G networks offer immense potential for entrepreneurs. By understanding how these technologies can be integrated into their business models, entrepreneurs can open up new avenues for growth and innovation.

Staying connected with industry leaders, attending technology conferences, and actively participating in entrepreneurial communities can provide valuable insights into emerging trends and technologies. Entrepreneurs should also foster a culture of experimentation and adaptability within their organizations, empowering employees to explore and embrace new technologies.

By regularly assessing the relevance and potential benefits of emerging technologies, entrepreneurs can position themselves at the forefront of innovation. Understanding how to implement these technologies effectively and ethically will allow them to shape their destiny and thrive in the ever-changing entrepreneurial landscape.

In Conclusion

The mission mindset of an entrepreneur is enriched by embracing technology and innovation. By leveraging disruptive technologies, embracing digital transformation, streamlining processes, collaborating globally, maximizing data and analytics insights, harnessing the power of AI, prioritizing cybersecurity, and navigating emerging technologies, entrepreneurs can shape their destiny in the entrepreneurial landscape.

The possibilities for growth, impact, and transformation are boundless for those who have the vision and the courage to embrace the rapidly evolving world of technology and innovation. Aspiring entrepreneurs, early-stage businesses, and change-makers can seize the opportunities that lie ahead by continually learning, adapting, and unlocking the transformative potential of technology.

In the relentless pursuit of their mission, entrepreneurs can reshape industries, create social change, and leave a lasting legacy. We invite you to step into the world of technology and innovation, where your destiny awaits.

Chapter 13

Financing and Funding Your Venture

E ntrepreneurship requires a delicate balance of passion, determination, and resources. While the former two are within your control, securing the necessary funds to support your entrepreneurial journey can often be a daunting task. As an aspiring entrepreneur, identifying and exploring various financing options, investment strategies, and funding sources is crucial to turn your dreams into reality. In this chapter, we will delve into the world of financing and funding, equipping you with the knowledge and tools you need to navigate the ever-changing landscape of entrepreneurial finance.

When it comes to financing your venture, the options are vast and diverse. Let's start by examining some of the most common avenues students, marketers, aspiring entrepreneurs, early-stage entrepreneurs, side hustlers, career changers, personal development enthusiasts, social and environmental change makers can consider.

1. Bootstrapping: Building from the Ground up

Bootstrapping, or self-funding, is perhaps the most straightforward way to finance your venture. This avenue involves utilizing personal savings, credit cards, or borrowing from friends and family to kickstart your entrepreneurial journey. While it may require sacrifices and discipline, bootstrapping provides you with complete control over your venture, ensuring you make all the critical decisions.

2. Angel Investors: Guidance and Support From Above

Angel investors are individuals who invest their own capital into early-stage ventures in exchange for equity. They not only provide financial support but also bring invaluable industry experience, guidance, and networks. Connecting with angel investors can be done through local networks, online platforms, or even by seeking out mentorship programs to tap into their wealth of knowledge and resources.

3. Venture Capital: Fueling High-Growth Potential

Venture capital (VC) firms, unlike angel investors, represent pooled funds from investors seeking high-potential, high-growth ventures to invest in. Typically, venture capitalists focus on technology-driven startups or those with disruptive business models. In exchange for funding, they take an equity stake in your venture and often actively participate in decision-making processes. Securing VC funding can provide your venture with significant capital injection, mentoring, and access to professional networks.

4. Crowdfunding: Harnessing the Power of the Crowd

The rise of digital platforms has revolutionized the concept of crowdfunding, allowing entrepreneurs to access capital from a wide audience. Crowdfunding platforms like Kickstarter, Indiegogo, or GoFundMe enable entrepreneurs to pitch their venture idea or prototype to the public, inviting individuals to contribute funds in exchange for various rewards or pre-orders of the product or service. Crowdfunding not only provides much-needed capital but also serves as a marketing strategy, validating your venture's concept and building a customer base from day one.

5. Business Incubators and Accelerators: Nurturing and Elevating Entrepreneurs

Business incubators and accelerators are organizations that provide support, guidance, resources, and, in some cases, funding to early-stage entrepreneurs. These programs typically run for a fixed period, during which entrepreneurs receive mentorship, access to shared office spaces, and connections to potential investors. Many incubators and accelerators focus on specific industries or sectors, catering to the diverse needs of entre-preneurs.

6. Grants and Competitions: Winning Support

Many organizations, including government entities, non-profit foundations, and corporations, offer grants and sponsor competi-tions aimed at funding innovative projects and startups. These grants and competitions not only provide financial support but also offer recognition, exposure, and validation for your venture.

Researching and identifying relevant grants and competitions can open doors to crucial funding and propel your entrepreneurial journey forward.

As you explore the various financing options available, it's essential to assess which aligns best with your venture's goals, capital requirements, and growth potential. Each option has its own advantages, challenges, and implications for equity ownership, decision-making power, and future fundraising efforts.

With this foundation in place, the next part of this chapter will delve deeper into investment strategies, funding sources, and financing structures. We will explore topics such as debt financing, equity financing, crowdfunding strategies, and building relationships with financial institutions. Stay tuned for more insights, as we continue to empower you with the knowledge and tools needed to shape your destiny as an entrepreneur.

Remember, this is just the first half of the chapter, and the journey to financing and funding your venture has only just begun. In the second half, we will dive into the nitty-gritty details and strategies that will help you navigate the complexities of entrepreneurial finance. Hang in there, and keep feeding your mission mindset. The best is yet to come.

As we dive deeper into the second half of this chapter on financing and funding your venture, we will continue to explore investment strategies, funding sources, and financing structures that can help you navigate the complexities of entrepreneurial finance. By equipping ourselves with the right knowledge and tools, we can better shape our destiny as entrepreneurs.

One investment strategy worth exploring is **debt financing**. Debt financing involves obtaining funds through loans or lines of credit, which must be repaid with interest over a specified period. This option allows you to retain full ownership and control of your venture while leveraging borrowed capital. It is important to carefully evaluate the terms and conditions of any debt financing options, ensuring that the interest rates and repayment terms align with your financial projections.

Equity financing, on the other hand, involves selling a portion of your venture to investors in exchange for capital. This approach allows you to access funds without incurring debt or interest payments. Equity financing can be an attractive option for high-growth ventures with substantial potential returns. However, it is crucial to consider the implications it may have on your ownership and decision-making power. Striking the right balance between equity and debt financing is a key consideration when evaluating financing options.

In addition to debt and equity financing, another avenue growing in popularity is **revenue-based financing**. This form of financing allows entrepreneurs to repay investors with a percentage of their monthly revenue until a predetermined return is achieved. Revenue-based financing can be an attractive option for ventures with consistent and predictable cash flow, as it aligns the investor's returns with the venture's performance.

Crowdfunding strategies also continue to evolve, presenting innovative ways for entrepreneurs to access capital. In addition to the traditional reward-based crowdfunding, newer models such as equity crowdfunding and Initial Coin Offerings (ICOs) have gained traction. Equity crowdfunding platforms provide a platform for entrepreneurs to sell shares of their venture to a crowd of individual investors. ICOs, on the other hand, involve issuing tokens or cryptocurrency in exchange for capital. These alternative crowdfunding strategies have the potential to democratize funding and open up new avenues for entrepreneurs.

Building **relationships with financial institutions** is

another crucial aspect of securing financing for your venture. Establishing strong connections with banks, credit unions, and other financial institutions can provide access to loans, lines of credit, and other financial products tailored to the needs of entrepreneurs. Networking with professionals in the finance industry, attending industry events, and seeking mentorship from experienced entrepreneurs can help you navigate the often complex landscape of financial partnerships.

It is also important to consider the implications of financing on your ventures' future fundraising efforts. Often, the choices made in the early stages of financing can impact your ability to raise capital in subsequent funding rounds. Assessing the short-term and long-term implications of financing options on your ventures' growth trajectory and equity ownership is crucial for making informed decisions.

As we conclude this chapter on financing and funding your venture, remember that the journey to securing capital to support your entrepreneurial dreams is a continuous process. It requires ongoing research, adaptability, and persistence. By staying informed about emerging financing options, regularly evaluating your ventures' financial needs, and seeking support from mentors and networks, you can position yourself for success.

Continue to feed your mission mindset, stay resilient in the face of challenges, and remain committed to shaping your own entrepreneurial destiny. With the right mindset, knowledge, and support, the best is yet to come on your entrepreneurial journey.

In the next chapter, we will explore the art of giving back to society and the environment. So, stay tuned as we continue to empower you on your path to entrepreneurial success.

Remember, the mission mindset is within your control, and the possibilities are endless.

Chapter 14

Giving Back: Social and Environmental Impact

As entrepreneurs, we have the power to shape our destinies and leave a positive impact on the world around us. Beyond the realm of profit and success lies the deeper purpose of giving back to society and the environment. In this chapter, we will embark on a journey to discover the significance of making a positive social and environmental impact through our entrepreneurial endeavors. We will also explore practical ways in which we can give back and create meaningful change.

In today's world, the concept of social and environmental responsibility has gained immense importance. People are becoming increasingly aware of the impact their actions have on the planet and society as a whole. As aspiring entrepreneurs, early-stage entrepreneurs, or even career changers, it is crucial for us to understand this significance and integrate it into our business models.

Social Impact: Creating Positive Change in Society

The power of entrepreneurship lies not only in our ability to innovate and create successful ventures but also in our capacity to positively influence society. By embracing a mission mindset, we can align our business goals with social causes and create a lasting impact.

One way to achieve this is through corporate social responsibility (CSR) initiatives, where businesses actively contribute to the betterment of society. These initiatives can range from donating a portion of profits to charitable organizations to engaging in community development projects. By incorporating CSR into their business strategies, entrepreneurs can build strong relationships with customers, employees, and the wider community.

Another avenue for making a social impact is through social entrepreneurship. Social entrepreneurs, motivated by a desire to solve pressing social problems, create innovative solutions that benefit society. These individuals leverage their entrepreneurial skills to address issues such as poverty, inequality, and lack of access to basic services. By harnessing their passion for social change, they drive transformation at the root level, creating ripple effects far and wide.

Environmental Impact: Promoting Sustainability and Conservation

In addition to social impact, entrepreneurs can also contribute to the preservation and conservation of our environment. As the effects of climate change become increasingly evident, environmental sustainability has emerged as a key concern for individuals and businesses alike.

One way to promote environmental impact is to adopt eco-friendly practices in our entrepreneurial ventures. This can include reducing waste, implementing energy-efficient measures, and opting for sustainable sourcing and production methods. By making conscious choices that minimize our carbon footprint, we can contribute to a healthier and more sustainable planet.

Moreover, environmental entrepreneurship offers a unique opportunity to combine our entrepreneurial spirit with our passion for environmental conservation. From developing renewable energy solutions to creating sustainable products, environmental entrepreneurs play a crucial role in shaping a greener future. By driving innovation in eco-friendly technologies and practices, they pave the way for a more sustainable and resilient planet.

Giving Back: Practical Ways to Make a Difference

Now that we understand the importance of social and environmental impact, let's explore some practical ways to give back through our entrepreneurial endeavors. Here are a few key approaches:

1. Cause-driven business models: Integrate a social or environmental mission into the core of your business. By aligning your values with your venture, you can create a business that is not only financially successful but also contributes to positive change.

2. Partnerships with nonprofits: Collaborate with organizations that are already working towards the causes you care about. By joining forces, you can amplify your impact and leverage their expertise and networks.

3. Product or service donations: Consider donating a percentage of your profits, products, or services to charitable organizations. This not only supports their work but also enhances your brand's reputation and customer loyalty.

4. Employee volunteer programs: Encourage your employees to volunteer their time and skills for social and environmental causes. By fostering a culture of giving back within your organization, you can create a sense of purpose and enhance employee engagement.

5. Education and awareness campaigns: Raise awareness about social and environmental issues through educational campaigns, events, or digital platforms. By increasing awareness, you inspire others to take action and contribute to positive change.

Remember, the choices we make today have the power to shape a better tomorrow. In the second half of this chapter, we will continue exploring practical strategies for giving back through our entrepreneurial endeavors. By implementing these approaches, we can make a tangible impact on society and the environment while pursuing our entrepreneurial goals.

6. Sustainable supply chain management: One critical aspect of achieving environmental impact is through sustainable supply chain management. This involves evaluating and improving the processes involved in sourcing, producing, and distributing our products or services. By ensuring that our supply chain practices align with sustainability principles, we can minimize waste, reduce greenhouse gas emissions, and promote responsible resource management. Additionally, working with suppliers who prioritize environmental sustainability further enhances our impact.

7. Impact investing: Impact investing refers to making investments that generate both financial returns and positive social or environmental outcomes. As entrepreneurs, we can leverage our resources and capital to support businesses or projects that address critical societal or environmental challenges. By actively seeking out impact investment opportunities, we can contribute to meaningful change while also benefiting financially.

8. Mentorship and knowledge sharing: Sharing our expertise and experiences with aspiring entrepreneurs or individuals from underprivileged backgrounds can be a powerful way to give back. By becoming mentors or offering educational programs, we can empower others to pursue their entrepreneurial dreams and equip them with the necessary skills to succeed. This approach not only fosters social empowerment but also creates a ripple effect of positive change in society.

9. Incorporating sustainability into marketing and communication: Entrepreneurs have a unique opportunity to utilize their marketing and communication channels to raise awareness about social and environmental issues. By highlighting our sustainable practices, eco-friendly products, or social impact initiatives, we can inspire others to follow suit. Engaging with customers through storytelling and showcasing the positive impact they can make through their purchasing decisions can also be effective in promoting change.

10. Advocacy and policy engagement: Entrepreneurs possess a powerful platform to advocate for policy changes that support social and environmental causes. By actively engaging with policymakers, participating in relevant forums, or joining industry associations, we can influence the development of policies and regulations that drive sustainable practices and address societal issues. Collaboration with other entrepreneurs and organizations further amplifies our collective voice and enhances our chances of driving meaningful change.

Throughout this chapter, we have explored the various ways in which entrepreneurs can give back and make a positive social and environmental impact. By adopting a mission mindset and integrating these strategies into our entrepreneurial journeys, we have the opportunity to create a world that is more sustainable, equitable, and prosperous.

As we conclude this chapter, it is crucial to remember that giving back is an ongoing commitment. It requires continuous learning, adaptability, and a genuine desire to create positive change. By staying informed about emerging social and environmental issues, regularly reassessing and improving our practices, and embracing collaboration, we can ensure that our entrepreneurial endeavors contribute to a better tomorrow.

Now, armed with the knowledge and inspiration gained from this chapter, it is time for you to embark on your own journey of social and environmental impact. Join the ranks of successful entrepreneurs who recognize the power they hold to shape destinies and create a lasting positive legacy. By infusing your entrepreneurial pursuits with a mission mindset, you can unlock a world of incredible possibilities.

Remember, your actions matter, and each step you take towards giving back counts. Together, we can build a future where entrepreneurship becomes a force for sustainable development, social progress, and a thriving planet.

Conclusion

As we conclude "The Mission Mindset: Shaping Your Destiny as an Entrepreneur," reflect on the journey we've undertaken together. The key lessons from each chapter form a mosaic of essential entrepreneurial wisdom—embracing a growth mindset, understanding the profound power of your 'Why', setting SMART goals, building resilience, mastering your time, strategically navigating risks, cultivating meaningful connections, accurately defining your audience, establishing a compelling brand identity, and articulating a value proposition that distinguishes you in the marketplace.

The path forward involves applying these lessons with intention and action. Assess your current position, align your business strategies with the insights gained, and step confidently into the realm of practical application. Experimentation and adaptation are your allies as you refine your approach based on real-world experiences and feedback. Remember, entrepreneurship is not just a career choice but a continuous journey of learning, growth, and self-discovery.

Conclusion

Armed with the knowledge from this book, you are more than ready to shape your destiny. Let your entrepreneurial spirit soar as you transform challenges into opportunities, vision into reality, and ambitions into achievements. The world awaits the unique contributions of your entrepreneurial venture. Forge ahead with a mission mindset, and let your journey inspire and impact the world around you.

∼

Also by R. Fredimann
Continue the series...

"Beyond Boundaries: Scaling Your Entrepreneurial Journey" continues the Side Hustle series, delving deeper into the strategies and mindset shifts necessary to transcend limitations and expand the scope of your entrepreneurial endeavors. This volume equips aspiring and established entrepreneurs with actionable insights and practical advice to navigate challenges, seize opportunities, and propel their businesses to new heights.

About the Author

An entrepreneur at heart, R. Fredimann embarked on a journey to financial independence, exploring various ventures from affiliate marketing to establishing an independent publishing company. Despite the challenges faced, the lessons learned have been invaluable, shaping a path towards creating impactful works that resonate with a global audience.